SHORT ·

ESKDALE

NORTH YORK MOORS

PAUL HANNON

waymaster

waymaster guides
Hillside Publications
12 Broadlands
Keighley
West Yorkshire
BD20 6HX

First Published 2003

© Paul Hannon 2003

ISBN 1 870141 70 9

Cover illustration: Baysdale
Back cover: Beggar's Bridge, Glaisdale
(Paul Hannon/Hillslides Picture Library)

Printed by Carnmor Print
95-97 London Road
Preston
Lancashire
PR1 4BA

CONTENTS

INTRODUCTION

Eskdale is the principal valley of the North York Moors, fourth largest of the National Parks in England and Wales. Designated in 1952 with an area of 553 square miles, it is the best-defined upland area of all, rising island-like from the surrounding plains and coast. The northern half of the Park is dominated by the Esk, a renowned salmon river, and the only one to flow east, entering the sea at Whitby. Its many tributaries are all ranged along its southern flank, and include Baysdale, Westerdale (the true head of Eskdale), Danby Dale, Little and Great Fryup Dales, Glaisdale and the Murk Esk valley. These dales are all short in length, with only the latter containing a sizeable village.

The main valley boasts a wealth of characterful villages serving as gateways to the side valleys. Resplendant with cottages boasting warm sandstone walls beneath red pantiled roofs, each village is surrounded by green fields, neatly packaged by drystone walls and hedgerows rising to an intake wall above which endless seas of heather roll beneath vast skyscapes. The presence of a railway station in most villages makes a rare feature, for the Esk Valley line provides the best mode of travel in a valley where many roads are narrow, winding and steep. These simple country halts present a rural scene little changed in half a century. Many villages are also served by bus, notably from Whitby.

The main side valley, that of the Murk Esk, leaves Eskdale at Grosmont, and runs south to the moorland village of Goathland. Now of celebrity status with the popularity of TV series *Heartbeat*, it has been longer known for the North Yorkshire Moors Railway that passes through. The Grosmont-Pickering section of the Whitby-Pickering Railway was closed by British Rail in 1965 (the Whitby-

Grosmont section was retained as part of the Esk Valley line), only to be saved by enthusiasts and re-opened in 1973. Today visitors can enjoy an 18-mile steam-hauled run through the very heart the moors, a memorable trip.

Eskdale is walkers' territory par excellence, with a plethora of challenging walks crossing it. Best known are the Lyke Wake Walk and the popular Coast to Coast Walk which finishes its journey here, while the spectacular Cleveland Way also skirts the area. While your rambles may be more modest adventures, they will nevertheless take you to a wealth of fascinating locations, with outstanding scenery, history and interest at every turn. Whilst the route description should be sufficient to guide you around each walk, a map is recommended for greater information: Ordnance Survey 1:25,000 scale maps give the finest detail, and Explorers OL26 and OL27 cover all the walks.

USEFUL INFORMATION

•North York Moors National Park
The Old Vicarage, Bondgate, Helmsley, York YO62 5BP
(01439-770657)
•The Moors Centre, Danby (01287-660654)
•Sutton Bank National Park Centre (01845-597426)
•Whitby Tourist Information (01947-602674)
•North Yorkshire Moors Railway
(01751-472508) (timetable 01751-473535)
•North Yorkshire Moors Association (01642-700535)
(working to protect the area's natural beauty)
•Ramblers' Association
2nd Floor, Camelford House, 87-89 Albert Embankment,
London SE1 7BR (020-7339 8500)
•Traveline - public transport information (0870-6082608)
•National Rail Enquiry Line (08457-484950)

ESKDALE
20 Short Scenic Walks

WHITBY

River Esk

A169

GUISBOROUGH

A171

A169

Percy Cross Rigg

Commondale

Hob Hole

Castleton

Ainthorpe

Danby

Westerdale

Esk

Lealholm

Little Fryup Dale

Glaisdale Rigg

Esk

Glaisdale

Egton

Egton Bridge

Grosmont

Beck Hole

Goathland

Hunt House

← N

Walk numbers

● Start points

O Other villages

8

A RECORD OF YOUR WALKS

WALK	DATE	NOTES
1		
2		
3		
4		
5		
6		
7		
8		
9		
10		
11		
12		
13		
14		
15		
16		
17		
18		
19		
20		

4¾ miles   from Percy Cross Rigg

**Apart from a short foray to a dramatic forest
viewpoint, this entire walk is on moorland,
with only minimal uphill work.**

•Start: *Surfaced terminus of minor road running north
(unsigned) from crossroads with Westerdale road off
Kildale-Commondale road (GR: 606118).*
•Map: *OS Explorer OL26, North York Moors West.*

Begin by heading back along the road's good
verge, dropping gently past the fenced site of an ancient
settlement. Clearly discernible here are five Iron Age hut
circles, thought to be two thousand years old and rare
examples for this corner of Yorkshire. The road itself has
much history too, being an ancient ridge road.

At the dip in the road a farm road descends left
for Sleddale. This is followed down to cross a bridge on
Codhill Slack, and up the other side to approach the gate
to the farm. This enviable location is a veritable island amid
the moors. Without entering, turn left on a broad track
slanting gently up the flank of Codhill Heights, a steady
rise with good views over the continuing northerly pastures
of this hidden valley. On the brow, vast heathery sweeps
instil a magnificent sense of space. Keep straight on the
improving grassy track to the edge of Guisborough Wood
plantations.

Here the course of the Cleveland Way is met. This
long-established National Trail runs a 109-mile course from
Helmsley to Filey Brigg, around three sides of the National

Park. Follow it through the gate into the trees. It runs briefly along the left edge before swinging right into the plantation to meet a forest road. Cross straight over and a short path runs to the edge of Highcliff Nab. At a guide-post just short of the cliff, the Cleveland Way ascends right to gain the airy crest.

At an altitude of some 1017ft/310m, this is very much a place to linger, taking in a rich and varied view. Highcliff Nab's substantial rock face protrudes from the claustrophobic covering of Guisborough Woods. The first feature of note is the bird's-eye prospect of Guisborough itself: hardly spectacular, but undeniably comprehensive. Keen eyes will pick out the lofty priory arch within its town centre location: though overrun by modern housing, you can still clearly trace the line of the former railway. Further north is the coastal town of Redcar to the right of the industrial sprawl of Teesside. Looking back, the tall obelisk of the Captain Cook Monument on Easby Moor overtops the moors beyond Highcliffe Farm.

Retrace steps to the gate back onto the moor, and turn right on the Cleveland Way as it drops down outside the wall dividing heather from the grassy pastures of Highcliffe Farm. Modern stone flagging is in evidence as it runs on, then leaves the wall towards the end. The clear path rises away then crosses the moor to meet what is the continuation of the Percy Cross Rigg road on Hutton Moor. Here it is a broad, rough road climbing out of the trees just down to the right.

Your way turns left on it, rising slightly and then running along to a red-brick wartime lookout shelter on the brow. From here the coast is seen behind Highcliff Nab, which overtops Highcliffe Farm's green fields beyond this sea of heather. The track then resumes gently downhill to the gate at the start of the tarmac.

4³4 miles   from Hob Hole

The unsung charm of secretive Baysdale is discovered by way of splendid moorland paths.

·Start: *Beckside parking area by ford at Hob Hole, on moorland road from Westerdale towards Kildale (GR: 652074).*
·Map: *OS Explorer OL26, North York Moors West.*

Hob Hole has long been a popular haunt of happy families, for picnicking and dabbling in the stream.

From the parking area strike northwards up the road, on a cruelly stiff climb with which to start a walk. It is enhanced however by immediately fine views into the unfolding valley of Baysdale. At a road junction turn left along a track, a fine way through the heather as it runs on at mid height through Baysdale, on the flank of Kildale Moor. This grand scenario continues for some time, running on past a wall corner to reach a path junction at a barn (the right branch climbs over the moor to Kildale). Advance straight along the wallside (gently uphill, very briefly), on a thinner path running along the bottom of the moor. When the wall drops away do likewise, resuming with it to reach a gate in it to finally leave the moor.

Through the gate descend through a gorse bank to a low barn. From here a faint track crosses to a bridge on Baysdale Beck to join an access road. Turn left to follow this up to The Low House. Named as Shepherds House on older maps, it boasts a very enviable location. Without entering its confines (the original path passed through the yard, but has been officially diverted from that shown on older maps), bear left on a rough track round the outside of a barn to a gate just above. Here a good track rises left into the trees, soon reaching a gate at the top.

Emerging onto open moor under Holiday Hill, the track continues rising to leave the adjacent plantation behind, and improves into a grassy track crossing the moor towards Great Hograh Beck. Just short of its tree-lined confines the track swings around to the right on a parallel course. Here locate a thin but clear path branching off left. This little gem runs closer to the gill and soon meets it at a superb point, where it is crossed by a delightful little arched bridge with an inscribed keystone bearing the date 1938. Alongside is a small memorial stone of more recent origin. The bridge marks the upper limit of the beck's enclosing foliage, which is emphasized by a sprawling, gnarled oak tree immediately beneath it.

Cross the bridge and ascend the other side to a prominent memorial cairn of 1981 atop a large boulder. Looking north-west across Baysdale the unmistakable tip of Roseberry Topping pierces a skyline very largely devoted to moorland. The cairned path (known as Skinner Howe Cross Road) now runs a memorable course across Great Hograh Moor, with glorious views over the valley. En route a minor dip crosses Little Hograh before dropping down over Little Hograh Moor to alight onto the cul-de-sac John Breckon Road as it crosses the moor. Westerdale village is seen ahead across its side valley, beneath the long arm of Castleton Rigg and the higher moors.

Turn left on this road down to a junction, and left again on the road's verges to slant back down to Hob Hole. Should the beck be in spate, a useful footbridge is available immediately downstream from the ford.

4³⁄₄ miles   from Westerdale

Sleepy Westerdale village guards the entrance to its own delectable valley, true birthplace of the Esk.

·Start: *Village centre (GR: 664058) roadside parking.*
·Map: *OS Explorer OL26, North York Moors West.*

Westerdale is the first village on the Esk, and gives its name to the dale's uppermost reach. This peaceful backwater is quieter still since the Victorian hall, once a shooting lodge, closed its doors to youth hostellers in 1992. At the bottom of the village is Hunter's Sty Bridge on the Esk, a centuries-old packhorse bridge bypassed by the road and with an old causey leading to it.

Leave the central junction beneath the church, on past the phone box to Westerdale Hall. Just past its grounds take a stile on the right, already with good open views over Westerdale's valley. Descend to a gate at the field bottom and drop to the bank of the Esk, then cross by a footbridge a few yards downstream. Turn upstream but quickly head away with a hedge to a gate, then ascend two field centres to the prominent Brown House. From a stile in front pass to the left of the house and through a gate into the field behind.

Turn left along the field bottoms to Stocking House, whose drive leads out onto the access road to Hawthorn House. Keep above all the buildings at this farm and a track runs to a gate. Resume across the field, the track soon fading but pointing the way to a gate part way up the far end. Here a faint path resumes to cross two field bottoms onto a corner of the open moor. In front are spoilheaps from old coalpits.

Advance a few yards to a grassy track that once served the workings, and turn down this to run along the wallside until unexpectedly joined by the terminus of a surfaced road ascending the field below. Keep straight on the continuing access track, a grand stride around to New House Farm, which appears on turning a corner. Don't advance to the farm itself, but take the second of two gates on the left. Looking updale, the Nab hovers over the dale's highest farm, aptly-named High House. Descend the large field to a gate at the end where wall and fence meet, then continue to a tiny footbridge on Stockdale Beck, just short of its confluence with the Esk.

Trace the youthful Esk upstream, leaving it to ascend a bank to meet Hill House farm road. Cross straight over to a stile in a hedge, then cross the field to Wood End. From the stile in front pass round to the right of the house to a stile in the corner. Across a tiny stone bridge, cross the field to a sturdier footbridge on a side-stream at its confluence with the Esk. A fading path runs beneath a steep bank to join High House farm road. Now turning for home, follow this left to ford the infant Esk.

As an enclosed lane the road climbs steeply to a junction with another drive at a gate beneath Waites House Farm. Fully surfaced, it continues pleasantly on (note the stone slab bridge at a ford). After ascending steeply beyond Riddings Farm to enter open moor, bear left off the road alongside the wall: a thin trod runs through bracken beneath recolonised spoilheaps. Further along, pass through a gate and swing left with the wall along a narrow enclosure. After a clearing reveals the church across a dip on the right, a firm path descends to cross the stream and rises up to the village hall and road.

—④——— HOB ON THE HILL

4 miles   from Commondale

**A largely linear walk to a historic moortop site,
with glorious heather surrounds.**

· Start: *Village centre (GR: 662105), roadside parking.*
· Map: *OS Explorer OL26, North York Moors West.*

Commondale nestles in apparent rural idyll among
rolling moors, though it was once dominated by a thriving
brickworks that supplied not so distant Teesside. One
glance around this small village illustrates how the bricks
were also put to local use (including the church on the hill
east of the village). Commondale has the *Cleveland Inn* pub,
a tearoom, WC and rail station (the westernmost in
Eskdale). All three roads leaving the village undertake
steep climbs, emphasizing the value of the railway.

Leave the village by climbing steeply west up the
Kildale road to arrive on the open moor. At once bear right
on an improving path across grassy moor. This quickly
arrives above Whiteley Beck, offering a brief choice of
paths. The first option descends immediately through
bracken, striding across the tiny stream and rising away on
a quickly improving path. Alternatively, remain on this side
as a superb flagged path suddenly appears and slants down
to the stream, halting then re-appearing in the bracken to
end abruptly at a twin slab bridge: now simply rise through
a few yards' thrash to join the clear main path.

The main path rises left across the heathery
slope to quickly ease out, running on into the side valley. It
soon turns again to slant up to the clear bank and dyke of

Park Pale, possibly a medieval deer park enclosure. This is followed left to join a shooters' track. Down to the left is the enviably sited farm of North Ings. Though the footpath crosses straight over, the actual point of departure from it to ascend to Hob on the Hill is indistinct in the extreme, so it is easier to bear right on the track, for now, and save that section of the path for the return, when it is easy to pick up.

For now then, take advantage of the track to the right, ascending very gently for just a few minutes until a small cairn on a level section indicates a thin branch to the right. The path ascends the flank of Skelderskew Moor past heather-camouflaged shooting butts. Across to the left are several distinctive stones, some in pairs: these trace the distinct bank of an ancient earthwork. The brow is soon gained, and just across to the left are several tumuli (ancient burial mounds). Of these, the most distinctive is crowned by a diminutive standing stone. This is Hob on the Hill, inscribed with its name and also with the initials and date *RC 1708*. This marks the summit and the turning point of the walk. The sweeping moorland panorama looks south to Eskdale and north to the coast. A 'hob', incidentally, was a mythical goblin-like character peculiar to the region: some were mischievous, others had healing powers.

Begin the return by retracing steps down to the track. This time however, simply cross it and descend through heather for only a minute to discover a thin but clear path. Turn left, soon reaching a tall standing stone, an evocatively sited memorial to two young friends who made the ultimate sacrifice in the Great War. Continue past this and an old railway guards van (recycled into a shooters' lunch cabin) to emerge back onto the track. Cross straight over onto the outward path alongside Park Pale dyke and bank, and retrace with pleasure the outward route.

4^{1}2 miles   from Commondale

A similar walk to the previous outing, but a different moorland objective best enjoyed in late summer.

· *Start: Village centre (GR: 662105), roadside parking.*
· *Map: OS Explorer OL26, North York Moors West.*

Commondale nestles in apparent rural idyll among rolling moors, though it was once dominated by a thriving brickworks that supplied not so distant Teesside. One glance around this small village illustrates how the bricks were also put to local use (including the church on the hill above the village). Commondale has the *Cleveland Inn* pub, tearoom, WC and rail station (Eskdale's westernmost).

Leave the village centre by climbing steeply west up the Kildale road to quickly arrive on the open moor. At once bear right on an improving path across grassy moor. This quickly arrives above Whiteley Beck, offering a brief choice of paths. The first option descends immediately through bracken, striding across the stream and rising away on a quickly improving path. Alternatively, remain on this side as a superb flagged path suddenly appears and slants down to the stream, halting then reappearing in the bracken. It ends abruptly at a slab bridge: now simply rise through a few yards' thrash to join the clear main path.

The main path rises left across the heathery slope to quickly ease out, running on into the side valley. It soon turns again to slant up to the clear bank and dyke of Park Pale, possibly a medieval deer park enclosure. This is followed left to join a shooters' track.

Down to the left is enviably sited North Ings Farm. Cross straight over the track (the return option) and resume along a thin path past a railway guards van recycled into a shooters' lunch cabin. A tall stone a little further is an evocatively sited memorial to two young friends, farm lads who enlisted as Grenadier Guards in the Great War, and made the ultimate sacrifice. Advance straight on the splendid little path, with the shooters' track never much more than a stone's throw above. The path however forges on regardless, passing through a line of stones of ancient origin. The pair nearest the path include one with a hollowed top put to use for leaving 'alms' (25p on my last visit). The stones trace a distinct bank, an ancient earthwork rising to the right.

The path rises gently away from the stream and onto the higher moor, ultimately arriving at another crossroads with the trusty track, just short of the brow. Prominent just yards to the left is the mound of a tumulus, an ancient burial site complete with a stone shelter. At 1076ft/328m, where Commondale and Gisborough Moors meet, this is a significant location as the highest point of the vast sweep of moorland on the north side of Eskdale. Oddly though, it appears of inferior altitude to the white Ordnance Survey column (324m) a mile to the north-west, in front of the plantations of Guisborough Woods. Either way, its grassy mound makes an ideal lunch halt. The very tip of Roseberry Topping peeps over the moor westwards, while a truly embracing panorama looks north-east to the coast.

The return options are simple: either retrace steps, or head back on the quality track. At the meeting point just past the old railway van, rejoin the outward footpath alongside Park Pale dyke and bank, to return as you came out.

4$\frac{1}{2}$ miles   from Castleton

The green floor of Danby Dale leads to the colourful flanks of a classic moorland ridge with superb views.

•Start: Village centre (GR: 686080), roadside parking
 or car park above village on old Westerdale road.
•Map: OS Explorer OL26, North York Moors West.

Once a market town, Castleton is the upper dale's principal village. The de Brus family built an 11th century wooden castle here, while the church has mouse carvings from the Kilburn workshops. An annual show is held each September. On the colourful slopes facing the village across the valley are the remains of inclined tramways that carried stone down from former quarries. Castleton boasts three pubs (*Downe Arms, Moorlands Inn, Eskdale Inn*), along with shops, Post office, tearoom, filling station, bank, rail station and WC.

Leave the main street by a drive (a bridleway) almost opposite the school. Over a brow it becomes grassy, descending to leave the village as an enclosed, sunken way dropping down into a field. Ahead is a fine prospect of Danby Dale, framed by Danby Rigg and Castleton Rigg, with the solitary Danby church straight ahead.

Cross to a gate across a tiny stream, then rise up the gentle brow with a hedge on the right. Follow this to the far end, through a corner gate across another stream-let. Up the bank behind turn right, a faint way running to another gate. Swinging left with the tiny stream, this remains your course for a direct march through several

18

gateways. At a gate in the first wall, the improving path swings left, on through several gates as it slants down to meet the main watercourse of the valley, Danby Beck.

The beck is followed upstream to a gate onto a T-junction. Go straight ahead on the no-through-road rising to West Green Farm. Advance the short way further to Plum Tree Farm, where the road promptly ends alongside an apt tree by the garden wall. At the house ignore the green track that replaces the road, and instead take a gate on the right to ascend the field alongside a sunken way. A gate at the top admits onto open moor: looking back, Danby Dale is at the heart of an all-embracing Danby scene, featuring Danby church, Danby Rigg, Danby village and on the slopes behind, Danby Beacon. The sunken way slants left, rising the short distance to meet the Hutton-le-Hole to Castleton road as it traverses Castleton Rigg.

Double back right on the accommodating grass verge for three-quarters of a mile, with Castleton village arrayed ahead. Before reaching a branch road a footpath sign sends an invisible path off to the right for a couple of heather bashing minutes. Meeting the minor road climbing out of Danby Dale, cross straight over onto a clear grassy path. This slants down the moorland flank, gradually levelling out before reaching the bottom to contour splendidly on through dense bracken.

At a fork above Forest Farm buildings, keep right to remain level a short way further to join a broad track. Bear left up this to run on to meet an access road. Resume along this, but just before it prepares to meet the road, an inviting little path bears right, contouring again towards a small wood ahead. A gate at the end admits onto the verge of the road just beneath a cattle-grid. Keep right on the verge round to the top of the village, just ahead, and finish down the main street with panoramic views over Eskdale.

4¹2 miles   from Castleton

**An undemanding ramble at the foot of Danby Dale
and along colourful moorland flanks.**

•Start: *Village centre (GR: 686080), roadside parking
or car park above village on old Westerdale road.*
•Map: *OS Explorer OL26, North York Moors West.*

For a note on Castleton, see Walk 6. Descend the
main street to the foot of the village and turn right on
Ashfield Road. This drops to cross Danby Beck and up to
open slopes beneath The Howe (Danby Low Moor on maps).
At a gate it leaves The Howe, and as Wandels Lane runs
along fieldsides. As it becomes enclosed Danby church
appears ahead, and a T-junction is quickly reached. Take
the stile in front and cross a field to the church.

St. Hilda's boasts a splendid, isolated setting in
the heart of Danby Dale. A 15th century tower looks up to
the high moors so loved by its famous incumbent, Canon J.
C. Atkinson. Vicar here for 53 years, his knowledge of local
life and history led to his classic work *Forty Years in a
Moorland Parish.* Laid to rest here in 1900, his grave is
marked by a stone cross twenty yards west of the tower.

Leave by the drive onto a road, going left to a
staggered crossroads. Turn right and follow this lane to a
fork. Bear right up to North End Farm. Immediately before
the house take a gate on the left, and ascend the fieldside
to a gate onto Ainthorpe Rigg's bracken flank. Turn left on
a smashing path above the wall, on sections of stone causey
and enjoying glorious views over Danby Dale to Castleton.

When the wall drops away contour straight on, and the wall soon returns. Just a few steps further, after a lone gorse bush, take a thin but clear grassy trod forking right.

This mercurial way gently ascends the moorland flank on lengthy sections of causey. At the top it rises as a hollowed way by old quarries, then a short grassy way through heather. Strictly, the vague continuing route is straight across the heather to join the clear course of a bridleway ascending Danby Rigg: if doing this, join it and turn left. In more common use is the clearer path swinging left above the heather colonised quarries. This slants down to join the bridleway a little lower. It then drops to a gate below, continuing down a grassy trough through dense gorse bushes to a road climbing out of Ainthorpe. Continue down this to the top of the village, where a nice green bearing quoits pitches fronts the *Fox & Hounds* pub.

Keep left down the green, and a grassy way drops down to a back road. Go left a few steps and take a stile on the left. A faint path heads off along the field bottoms, through a succession of stiles to a farmyard. Follow the short track out onto a road, Longlands Lane. Go left just as far as Danby Vicarage, then take a stile on the right. Past a garden bear right to a wall-stile, then slant up to the top corner of the large field. Confusingly, ignore the splendid old stile by the gate, and take a ladder-stile in the corner. Ascend the fieldside to a gate into the yard of Howe Farm.

Rise to the cattle-grid and follow the access road away past a restored well and along the base of The Howe towards a road. Don't join it but take a grassy path left to Castleton's war memorial, which records no fewer than 26 local men lost their lives in World War One. The lower path leaving it curves down to a footbridge on Danby Beck. Up the other side an enclosed footway rises to the road directly beneath the church. Turn left for the centre.

4^{1}2 miles   from Ainthorpe

Bracing walking along Eskdale's finest moorland ridge contrasts with the sylvan charm of Little Fryup Dale.

•*Start: Minor road onto the moor just south of the pub (GR: 706073), firm verge parking, notably by village sign.*
•*Map: OS Explorer OL27, North York Moors East.*

Follow the road climbing to the moor, ignoring any paths until beyond the tennis courts. As the road swings left take a bridleway ahead, a grassy trough rising through dense gorse to a gate onto Danby Rigg. Known as Old Wife's Stone's Road, the path maintains a gentle ascent through heather. Part way, you pass a massive stone dominating a ring of small stones, once part of a large circle around an important burial cairn, possibly 3000 years old.

The well defined eastern edge of the rigg is gained dramatically, a magnificent moment overlooking Little Fryup Dale. The bridleway drops away here, and can be followed down to the road should grouse shooting be taking place. Otherwise, a concessionary path remains on the edge to savour a splendid tramp. An old road (merely a track) is crossed, passing an Ordnance Survey column and adjacent standing stone over to the right. Danby Rigg is renowned for bearing hundreds of small, ancient burial cairns, several of which might be spotted amongst the heather. Its views are equally impressive, a particularly interesting aspect looking west to the celebrated pairing of the Captain Cook Monument on Easby Moor and the peak of Roseberry Topping.

The edge path quickly encounters another ancient earthwork, Double Dyke which cuts through the path. Just a little further is a line of shooting butts, past which a cairn marks a crossroads with an old track known as Jack Sledge Road. Double sharply back left on a smashing path that angles down towards the open road below. On joining it turn left on the verge to a junction in Little Fryup Dale.

Leave by the road off the moor, becoming enclosed at a cattle-grid to drop to cottages at Stonebeck Gate. Up the other side, turn left along the house front at Stonebeck Gate Farm. This access road emerges into fields to run to the isolated Forester's Lodge. Dropping towards the house, take a gate to the right and slant down the field. From a gate in the bottom wall, an ill-drained little way leads out into another field. An old green track heads away, then slants down to the corner. Little Fryup Beck is bridged and an enclosed cart track climbs away to a gate onto open moor. Ascend the wallside path onto the open road.

Go right to the enviably sited Crossley Gate Farm, above which an inviting path ascends the steep bracken bank to the brow above. Pause to survey a glorious view: the head of neighbouring Great Fryup Dale is glimpsed beyond the more complete prospect of Little Fryup Dale at your feet, while Houlsyke's cluster of red roofs is prominent down Eskdale. The path now heads grandly off through heather. Old views return, with Danby to the right alongside the Clitherbeck side valley: just as quickly, straight ahead, Castleton appears with Roseberry Topping behind.

The little path encourages good strides until above the hollow of The Coombs, its green fields beyond a wall. At a cairn remain on the main path slanting down to the right. It briefly shadows a ditch, but as that drops away remain on the path bearing left, down to rejoin the outward path. Turn back down through gate and gorse to finish.

3³⁄₄ miles   from Danby

**A historic trading route is traced
across colourful moorland slopes.**

•*Start: Village centre crossroads, parking area
just east of pub on Lodge Lane (GR: 707086).*
•*Map: OS Explorer OL26, North York Moors West.*

Danby's focal point is Dale End crossroads. Here
are found the *Duke of Wellington* pub, bakery/tearoom and
Post office/shop. Just down the road are the rail station
and WC. There is a fine tradition of beekeeping locally,
while Danby is also known for being the location of one of
the last remaining Courts Leet, a relic from manorial days
when villagers meet to decide local issues.

Head down the street towards the station, but
turn right at Bridge Green past a Methodist chapel - note
the 1811 sundial on the old school alongside. Across a
bridge rise on a short-lived access road above the stream,
accompanied by a stone causey. Towards the top take a
stile in the adjacent wall, and an enclosed path runs to a
gate into a field. Cross the field bottom to a stile in a tiny
section of wall, and from a stile just beyond, head across a
sloping field to a corner gate. Turn immediately uphill to a
stile onto the Castleton road.

Go left a short way along the road, and as it opens
out and starts to drop away, take a grassy way on the right.
This crosses an access road then runs as a broad track into
bracken-clad slopes. The river shimmers down to the left,
with Danby Rigg and Danby Dale beyond. Castleton Rigg and

village soon enter the scene ahead. Stride out to reach a distinct junction. Fork right and ascend to a wall corner.

Don't enter the island field but ascend right to a gate, from where a hollowed green way continues up under an old hedge. Underfoot is the Pannierman's Causeway, one of countless old trade routes that thread the valley sides and moors of Eskdale. Continue beyond this across heather moor to a gate in a fence opposite. Now just a path, the way bears left over diminishing moor to the far corner, merging into a broader green track just short of the gate. A splendid walled way now runs to a gate back onto moorland.

Turn right on a grassy way descending the wallside, and towards the bottom a gate sees you back off the moor and doubles back, enclosed, along the wood top. This then drops to a ford and stepping-stones on the little beck. Rise away with a sidestream to a gate, then ascend the field towards the house at Rosedale Intake. Pass through a gate at the top, then rise left back onto heather moor. A clear path ascends, easing out to reach a path crossroads.

Go straight across on a good, level path showing evidence of old stone causeway. As it swings further left a sustained section of stone causeway is enjoyed before it reverts to moister terrain to slowly merge into a moorland road. Go left on the verge for 250 yards to a minor bridge, which marks the turning point. Double sharply back to the right to commence the return on a broad track known as the Lord's Turnpike. To the left is the side valley of Clitherbeck, across which are the slopes of Danby Beacon.

This track runs infallibly across the moor to a wall corner. Bear right here to a track junction, and take that straight ahead, with Danby just below. This drops quickly down to a gate off the moor. A good track continues down a gorse pasture to emerge onto the road on the edge of the village, with the crossroads just along to the right.

4¹2 miles   from Danby

**The colourful side valley of Clitherbeck ultimately
leads to a superb packhorse bridge and ruined castle.**

•Start: The Moors Centre (GR: 716084)
Danby Lodge car park, half a mile east of village.
•Map: OS Explorer OL27, North York Moors East.

Originally a shooting lodge, Danby Lodge is now a
National Park visitor centre, with information, displays,
café and shop. From the road junction outside the Lodge,
take a gate into woodland. A broad path ascends beneath
tall beeches to a gate into open pasture overlooking
Clitherbeck. A grassy way rises alongside the wall, but
quickly bear away and slant down to a gate into an enclosure
of newly planted trees. Quickly emerging at the other end,
advance through a gateway in a wall and along a flat field.

Joining the beck (with a pond just across it) pass
through a gate to a ford and footbridge. Across, a good
path turns upstream through scattered oaks to a ladder-
stile. The path now begins a steady slant away from the
beck, a fine traverse across bracken flanks. With good
views over this valley it ultimately meets a wall corner.

Double back to the right, initially unconvincingly
to trace an improving trod on a near-level course.
Immediately above are spoilheaps of the Castleton Pits
coal workings (note that just above these remains is the
firm track you will shortly join). The trod, meanwhile, runs
a clear course across the moor, eventually slanting up to a
tiny stream. The track is just a few steps further up. Turn

right past further spoilheaps and out to a junction with the road descending from Danby Beacon.

Cross straight over and along the broad verge of a minor road, through scant evidence of RAF Danby World War Two radar station. The road drops to another junction at the end. At the gate in front leave the moor to descend a walled track through Oakley Sides to a back road. Turn right, soon zigzagging downhill and then along to pass under a railway bridge to join the main valley road. Go right, briefly, then bear left along a side road to Duck Bridge. This shapely arched packhorse bridge on the Esk has 14th century origins, yet it was only as recently as 1993 that it was finally retired upon construction of the adjacent ford.

Across the bridge ascend left to a T-junction. To the left is Danby Castle, 14th century fortified home of the Latimers. Its best known resident was Catherine Parr, one of Henry VIII's favourite half-dozen. The appreciable remains are intertwined with farm buildings still very much in use, and the north-west tower is particularly well seen from the roadside: it enjoys a fine prospect over mid-Eskdale. Back at the junction turn on the top road, quickly taking a gate on the right. Descend a fieldside track past an island barn to the rear of Castle Houses farm, where go left on a cross-field track to a gate. Slant down to a gate in the far corner, then cross the field to the hedge at the far side. Turn left to a corner kissing-gate, then right along the hedge to a stile onto a back road at Kadelands.

Turn right for a short while above an attractive section of the Esk, then take a gate on the left and descend the fieldside to the railway line. Across, head away with an old fence on the left, on to a footbridge on the river. Across the field behind, a stile admits to Danby Lodge grounds, or go straight ahead to the road opposite the car park.

4$\frac{1}{4}$ miles   from Danby

**A rich tapestry of paths and byways lead
to and from a celebrated Eskdale viewpoint.**

•*Start: The Moors Centre (GR: 716084)
Danby Lodge car park, half a mile east of village.*
•*Map: OS Explorer OL27, North York Moors East.*

Danby Lodge was originally a shooting lodge of the
Dawnays. It now serves as a visitor centre for the National
Park, with information, displays, café and shop. From the
car park head left (east) along the road a short way as far
as a stile in the hedge on the left. Slant half-right to the
field top, then bear right along to a stile above Park House.
Joining an enclosed cart track, follow this uphill and along
to High Butterwitts Farm. Pass all the buildings (note the
series of three stone water troughs) and out onto a hairpin
bend of a narrow lane. Bear left here, quickly levelling out
to run along the valley side. This grand stride on a traffic-
free byway enjoys big views over the dale.

As the roofs of Houlsyke appear below, turn left
at a short-lived track into trees. The path crosses straight
over it and up to a ladder-stile into a field. Steeply ascend
the wallside on the left. From a gate at the top pause to
look back over a wide sweep of the valley: across are Great
and Little Fryup Dales, while downdale the wooded ravine
of Crunkly Gill sits beneath the skyline 'sandcastle' at RAF
Fylingdales. The gate admits to a broad, walled way,
through which a good path rises to a gate onto open moor,
with a minor road just above.

Turn right on the wide verge, above the isolated Oakley Walls Farm and along to where a gate on the right sees a surfaced road ascend steeply from Houlsyke. Don't take it, but instead turn left up a track alongside a sunken way onto the moor. Rising by a few rocks and shooting butts, you will quickly espy the white Ordnance Surve column and roadsign indicating the location of Danby Beacon. The old way rises gently across the moor to emerge onto a hairpin bend of the road at the Beacon.

At 981ft/299m, Danby Beacon was one of a chain of beacon sites where a fire could spread word of impending danger, or help celebrate some notable event. The hilltop is crowned by a distinctive tumulus, an ancient burial mound. A modern view indicator identifies a wide panorama in which natural features are equalled by man-made efforts, including Boulby Potash Mine on the coast, Scaling Dam, Captain Cook's Monument on Easby Moor, Bilsdale mast and RAF Fylingdales.

Turn left on the cushioned grass verge of the road descending across the moor, with little traffic and superb vistas over the upper dale: note also the extensive seascape northwards. Towards the bottom ignore a branch road left, and instead, approaching a wall on the right, turn along a grassy way on its top side. This runs on the moor bottom to the wall's corner, then descend with it into the side valley of Clitherbeck.

At the bottom turn briefly upstream to a foot-bridge with a stile behind, and a path crosses to a distinct grassy path in front. Turn left on this, passing through an enclosed area of newly planted trees. Quickly leaving again, slant across the sloping pasture towards the top wall, where a grassy path runs down to a gate into a wood. A broad path drops down through tall beeches to a gate onto the road junction outside Danby Lodge.

3³⁄₄ miles   from Little Fryup Dale

A simple stroll in the lovely surroundings of the unfrequented valley of Little Fryup Dale.

•*Start: Little Fryup Dale (GR: 710055), 1¹⁄₂ miles south of Danby Castle, reached from Ainthorpe. Parking area at road junction.*
•*Map: OS Explorer OL27, North York Moors East.*

Ignoring tempting ways up onto Danby Rigg, take the Fryup road down off the moor. Across a cattle-grid it becomes enclosed to descend to the cottages at Stonebeck Gate and up (note a section of stone causey on the left) to Stonebeck Gate Farm. Continue up past the farm, this time noting a series of three adjacent stone troughs. A little further up, a bridleway leaves through a gate on the left. This grassy way runs pleasantly between walls, steadily ascending to then run on to a junction behind a gate.

Here turn right, ascending an improved green way to a gate beneath a stand of pines at the top. The track then runs left, through a bracken bank now extensively planted with a mix of native trees. This is a fine stride, looking across tranquil Little Fryup Dale to Danby Rigg. Towards the end the way rises to a gate onto the edge of the moorland crown of Heads. This upturned boat of a hill divides Great and Little Fryup Dales, a colourful and very tranquil backwater better known as Fairy Cross Plain.

Just a few steps further, the fence enclosing the plantings drops away and the path forks. Little Fryup Dale can be appraised in its modest entirety below, while also on view are Danby Castle (amid farm buildings at the northern foot of Danby Rigg), Danby village, the side valley of Clitherbeck, and Danby Beacon. From this fork an inviting branch continues straight on the edge, but this is not the true way. The actual bridleway forks right, to commence a delightful ramble across the centre of this pleasant upland.

Soon there is another fork in the heather. While this commonly used path contours straight on, the true way again forks right: initially vague, it rapidly appears as a green way through dense heather. Again grand underfoot, it runs purposefully on with a parallel wall quite close by. When the heather fades, so does the path. Bear left back down the gentle slope past a lone holly to rejoin the middle way. This continues to the wall ahead before swinging left to a gate, now back above the Little Fryup edge. With a mere green field through the gate, this is the turning point.

Double back fifty yards to a gate in the fence along the edge. Through this a splendid old pathway slants down the bank consisting largely of gnarled oaks, at the bottom doing a small zigzag through new plantings to a gate where wall and fence meet below. Slant down this rough pasture to a grassy track along the bottom, and turn left to a corner gate. Remain on this track, incorporating an enclosed section, to run on to meet the access road serving the isolated group of buildings at Forester's Lodge.

Dropping towards the house, take a gate in front of it and slant down the field. From a gate in the bottom wall, a poorly drained little way leads out into another field. An old green track heads away, then slants to the bottom corner. Here tiny Little Fryup Beck is bridged and an enclosed cart track climbs away to a gate onto open moor. Ascend the wallside path onto the open road. Turn left along here to finish, enjoying grassy verges all the way back to the start, beneath Danby Rigg's colourful edge.

-(13)——— GREAT FRYUP HEAD

4¹⁄₂ miles   from Glaisdale Rigg

**A walk into the enchanting head of Great Fryup Dale
is an experience that really should not be missed.**

• *Start: Hart Leap (GR 734035), in a depression on the
moorland road to Rosedale, almost four miles south-west
of Lealholm. Limited roadside parking, but more space
available on sections of verge in the half-mile further
south, which is, conveniently, the walk's last half-mile.
Best parking is a small parking area on road
climbing north from Hart Leap.*
• *Map: OS Explorer OL27, North York Moors East.*

        Why Hart Leap? Well, fifty yards from the road,
and some ten yards apart, is a pair of stone posts supposed
to mark the final, enormous leap of a hunted deer: the one
nearest the road is inscribed *Hart Leap*. Of various routes
departing Hart Leap, put your faith in the footpath sign
pointing north-west. Descending the moor it is possible to
locate the thin trod as it drops to a wall which appears only
minutes below. Across the ladder-stile, steep ground
reveals the floor of Great Fryup Dale directly below, with
Fairy Cross Plain and Danby Rigg beyond. Next objective is
the sprawling farm at Applegarth beneath your feet.
        Bear a little left down the steep, bracken slope to
avoid the deep confines of a gill, and a thin trod can be
carefully traced down to grassier terrain. A small gate in
the wall below leads into a large field. Slant to the bottom
left corner, with a stile onto a narrow back road. Go left,
keeping straight on when the through road forks right.

The road ends at a nice range of vernacular out-buildings at Fryup Lodge. Keep straight on the track past the buildings to a bridge over Great Fryup Beck. A rougher track continues up-dale through several fields to the barns at Dale Head. Pass right of them, and immediately beyond, turn right to ascend by a tiny stream. Behind a collapsed wall at the top, a fence-stile leads onto a level path. Go left on this as it runs more faintly above a wall and beneath the curiously intriguing knolls of The Hills. In front is the moody, charismatic dalehead, with the waterfall at Yew Grain Scar visible. When the wall/fence drops away the faint path runs on to a gate in an intervening wall.

Now firmly in the amphitheatre under Great Fryup Head, the path drops to cross little Trough Gill Beck in a truly lovely corner. The way doubles back right up the steep little bank behind, then ascends more directly through bracken to cross another tiny stream. This it follows up the increasingly steep slope before doubling back left for a short, steep pull up a good path out of the valley head. The dalehead oozes character, this final climb being hemmed in by rugged, colourful slopes. The path underfoot is the George Gap Causeway, an old moorland crossing to Rosedale.

Above some outcrops the gradient suddenly eases. Here advance with care a few steps further along the grassy edge to reveal the waterfall tumbling down Yew Grain Scar, amid evidence of landslips. Back on the path, meanwhile, it gently rises, grassy again, across the moor to quickly meet a wide path at a large cairn. Turn left on this well used way (known as the Cut Road, and followed by the Coast to Coast Walk) across Glaisdale High Moor, retaining good views into Great Fryup Dale for a considerable time. Ahead, the surfaced road is seen climbing above Hart Leap, long before joining it. At this point the valley of Glaisdale appears outspread ahead. Go left on the verge to finish.

4¹2 miles   from Lealholm

**Varied walking from riverbank to moorland, crowned
by a stride along a classic stone causeway.**

• *Start: Village centre car park (GR: 763076).*
• *Map: OS Explorer OL27, North York Moors East.*

        Lealholm is a hugely attractive village on a lovely
stretch of the Esk: a fine stone bridge is supplemented by
well-used stepping-stones just upstream. Alongside the
bridge is a spacious green on which Eskdale's 'national
game' of quoits is played. Adjacent churches (one Roman
Catholic) face each other on the climb to the station: there
is also a fine Wesleyan Chapel of 1839, with an old Quaker
burial ground close by. Other facilities include the *Board
Inn*, a shop, Post office, tearoom, pottery, WC and garage.
        A rough road leaves the foot of the car park to
run past a cottage into open country above the Esk. Remain
on this, above the river, all the way to Underpark Farm.
Entering the yard turn swiftly right and around to a stile
out into a field. Head downstream on a riverside flood
embankment, the path ascending a wooded bank at the end.
Alongside the railway a rough road is joined descending
from the rail bridge. Turn down this and round to a ford
and footbridge on the river, immediately upstream of a rail
viaduct. Don't cross the Esk but continue downstream to a
stile and a few steps further beneath the rail bridge arch.
        Now leave the river by turning sharp left to
ascend the fieldside, quickly passing through a stile alongside the railway. Continue directly up towards Park House,

using a gate in the corner on the right. Ascend past all the farm buildings (house doorway has a 1693 lintel). At the top barn turn left above it, but halfway on this patch of rough ground locate a stile in the hollies above. Ascend to a gate with Hill House Farm just above, but turn left on its drive to drop down to Rake Lane. Turn right up this road, then as it climbs steeply beyond a dip, take a signed path up through bracken on the right to a stile. Ascend the field-side above a minor side valley, being joined by a fence on almost levelling out. Field boundaries hereabouts have vanished in attempts to create a sloping version of East Anglia.

From this corner bear right over the brow to meet a firm track in the far corner. Cross over it to a simple bridge and ascend the hedgeside, left. When a wall takes over pass to the other side to follow it to a gate at the top. Cross to a gateway in a section of wall ahead and bear right with the fence to a gate onto moorland. Go right a few yards on the grassy track towards the corner, but then turn left on a thin but good path along the edge of the heather. At a gate off the moor at the end, continue straight on the fieldside to a road junction at Stonegate.

Double back left on the Lealholm road, quickly bearing right on a rough moorland road. Rising gently away, leave this even more rapidly at a path signed to the left. This contrasting little gem rises away over Lealholm Rigg, quickly becoming a superb stone causey. This remains intact all the way to a standing stone on the brow. Just a couple of steps beyond the stone, turn left on a thin trod down the grassy rigg to a road junction above Lealholm Side. Now simply head down the road for a steep finish back into Lealholm. At a junction stands a stone memorial to two US airmen killed in a plane crash here in 1979. Below this point a stone causeway adds interest before dropping down over the railway bridge and back to the start.

4 miles   **from Glaisdale**

The old road of Glaisdale Rigg perfectly complements the green floor of Glaisdale's own valley.

• *Start: Head of a cul-de-sac road from The Green (a grassy triangle) at top of village. The road rises to lose its surface at a gate onto the moor: parking on verge before gate (GR: 769053).*
• *Map: OS Explorer OL27, North York Moors East.*

Glaisdale village spreads from Beggar's Bridge over the Esk up to the edge of Glaisdale Rigg. Standing at the end of its own side valley, Glaisdale boasts both lovely woods and rolling moors on its doorstep. Though peaceful enough today, the village was a scene of great activity when caught up in the 19th century iron ore boom. Though the *Anglers Rest* has recently closed, two pubs, the *Mitre Tavern* and the *Arncliff Arms*, remain. There is also a Post office/shop, butcher, filling station, rail station and WC.

Pass through the gate onto Glaisdale Low Moor and ascend the firm track, an old road beginning its long haul onto Glaisdale Rigg. Rising only gently it soon arrives at a reedy pool. Behind is the embankment of a mineral tramway built to serve quarries which you will shortly pass.

Just beyond the pool as the road starts to rise away, fork left on an inviting grassy bridle-track. This runs on with fine views of Glaisdale's own side valley opening up from these colourful moorland flanks. Pass beneath an island pasture now used by equestrians, and above the rim of an old quarry draped in gorse, one of a string along the moorside here. The track then drops to reach a cross-tracks alongside a stone arched bridge. Continue across to become enclosed by walls just a little further down. Through a gate the green way drops down onto the road along Glaisdale Side. On the left is a splendid Methodist Chapel of 1821. Across the road is the long range of Postgate Farm, a name recalling Father Nicholas Postgate, 'Martyr of the Moors' (see Walk 16).

Turn right on this pleasant road along Glaisdale Side, noting the stone causeway regularly appearing in the verge. Known as the Monks' Trod, it was used by ponies laden with goods when its surface would have been superior to the road. The valley of Glaisdale was an important trade route, several farm names reflecting more distant places. Walk for three-quarters of a mile until the third bridleway on the right, shortly after passing Bransdale Farm.

Your way out of the valley is up the inviting finger of bracken-filled moorland reaching down. Rise to the gate and ascend the grassy path up the flank, swinging right to a wall corner at the top before easing out to head across the moor, gently rising to meet the unmistakable course of the Glaisdale Rigg old road. From this high point at 985ft/300m, all that remains is turn down this to follow it back to the start. Long, uncomplicated strides on this firm surface leave you free to savour the massive Eskdale views.

Of particular attention, part way down, is a superb early 18th century guidestone set into a socket. This comes just before a junction with a like track, and stands firmly on the roadside. It is inscribed on all sides with placenames, two of which were too long to fit on one line! Further, as the road makes a gentle rise, twenty yards to the left, just before the brow is a 1967 memorial to someone who "loved the moors", which has found its way onto the map. Beyond this the road soon drops down to the pool, and then the end.

16 — EGTON BRIDGE

4 miles **from Glaisdale**

Two historic routes linked along the floor of Eskdale in a linear walk taking advantage of the Esk Valley line to return - it might be more practical to begin at Grosmont, and catch the train to Glaisdale to start.

- *Start: Village centre (GR: 783055), parking by Beggar's Bridge, also small station car park.*
- *Map: OS Explorer OL27, North York Moors East.*

From the station, Beggar's Bridge is hidden behind the low railway viaduct: pass under it to view the graceful arch high above the Esk. Dating from the early 1600s, it served the packhorse era (Walk 15 has more on Glaisdale). Return to the road and leave by a footbridge into East Arnecliff Wood. The path climbs steeply, nears the river, then climbs again on a long section of paving. This centuries-old pannierway is one of the best known and most used of many such trade routes that criss-cross Eskdale. The woodland walk is one of great variety: the high-level path avoids the steep drop to the river, though the Esk can occasionally be glimpsed in lively mood.

A gentler conclusion leads out onto a back road: turn downhill for Egton Bridge. This quiet lane gives nice views over the Egton Grange side valley, and across the main valley to the red roofs of Egton village high on the slopes beyond. The village is entered at the *Horseshoe Hotel* (public bar). At a T-junction just past it, go down steps to the river, crossing by dependable stepping-stones in two sections. Up onto a road, turn right to a junction between church and bridge, just past the WC. If the river be in flood, remain on the road to the bridge.

Secreted in a lovely corner of Eskdale, Egton Bridge is rich in natural and historical attractions. It was the birthplace of Nicholas Postgate, 'Martyr of the Moors', who spent many post-Reformation decades in this strongly Catholic district. Finally apprehended in 1679, he was hanged, drawn and quartered on the Knavesmire at York, an old man of 82. His memory is perpetuated by a pub, and his faith by St. Hedda's church, built in 1866 and famed for its exterior bas-relief panels of scenes from the life of Christ: inside are relics of Father Postgate. The *Postgate Inn* stands by the station. A celebrated Gooseberry Show is held here in August.

Depart Egton Bridge by a rough road opposite the church, an Egton estates permissive route. If the mileage to Grosmont is still only '1', then it's fibbing. Early on, glance back to see the large house of Egton Manor. This former toll road runs along the valley floor of the Esk, passing Beckside Farm and a surviving notice of tolls affixed to the old toll-cottage. The road passes under a railway bridge and concludes by the riverside before emerging onto a road on the edge of Grosmont. Turn right over the imposing river bridge into the village.

Grosmont sits at the foot of numerous steep roads. Dominated in the 19th century by ironstone mining, there is less to see of earlier times, when, as Growmond, it supported an abbey of the Grantimontine order. Today railways take centre stage, as the Esk Valley line meets the preserved North Yorkshire Moors Railway, each with its own station. Hard by the level crossing is the *Station Tavern*, also tearooms, Post office, shops (including Grosmont's very own long-established Co-operative store) and WC.

4¹₂ miles   from Grosmont

A picturesque hidden hamlet in steam train country.

- *Start: Village centre (GR: 827052), two car parks.*
- *Map: OS Explorer OL27, North York Moors East.*

Leave Grosmont (see Walk 16) on a surfaced path by the level crossing, opposite the signal box. It crosses the Murk Esk on a footbridge parallel with the railway bridge, then forks. That straight ahead goes under the tunnel to the rail sheds, but instead fork left up past the church. Rise to a gate at the top, turning right to climb to a seat with a fine view over the village. Here turn through a gate on the left, on an enclosed path past the sheds and down to run parallel with the line. Soon a gate gives access to the track of the old line, and resume on that, parallel with the present line.

The railway between Pickering and Grosmont was completed in 1836 as a horse-drawn tramway. A decade later it was improved to take steam locomotives. A steep incline operated from Beck Hole to Goathland, but its deficiencies resulted in construction of a deviation line between Grosmont and Goathland. Opened in 1865, the replacement improved the gradient by beginning its climb earlier. The abandoned line now serves as this footpath.

The track runs on to Esk Valley, whose terraces housed workers in the local 19th century ironstone mines. Advance through a gate ahead, a much-improved track on the old line through the Murk Esk's wooded surrounds. The Murk Esk is the largest tributary of the Esk, formed by the confluence of West and Eller Becks at Beck Hole. The river is crossed by a footbridge on railway supports, continuing into woodland where a bridge re-crosses the river. Don't cross this one, but remain on the bank on a good path that shadows the river, then continues straight on the wood bottom to emerge into Beck Hole. This sleepy hamlet enjoys an enchanting setting, with a quoits pitch on the green and an oil painting inn sign. The *Birch Hall Inn* is a gem, and doubles as a small shop!

The route turns sharp left up the steep road out of the hamlet. Crossing a bridge on the present railway at the top, it rises away, easing out onto open moor beneath large spoilheaps from old ironstone workings. Remain on the verge until a roadside phone box, where a cul-de-sac lane descends a reedy moorland finger. At the bottom turn right to a gate above Green End Farm, and cross a small enclosure to a gate. Advance on here to become enclosed by hedgerows, a length of stone causey helping through a potentially muddy section. Emerging at a gate, fork right down a grassy path into trees, crossing a bridge and heading away through the wood. At the end a sloping field top is crossed to a stile back into woodland. However, the path simply curves up to a stile straight back out, to run along a field bottom above the wood. At the far end are a stile/footbridge into Crag Cliff Wood.

A splendid path heads away, steadily losing height and encountering good sections of causey. These lead to a gate out of the wood, and remain in place to point down the field onto a rough road. Turn down this, briefly into woods and emerging to reveal Grosmont ahead. Approaching a ford on the Murk Esk bear left to a footbridge on the beck, and rise on an enclosed path to the church. Stiles send a short-cut through the yard to rejoin the opening steps just two minutes from the start.

4 miles   from Goathland

Rich attractions of a steam railway and a waterfall.

·*Start: Village centre (GR: 833012), car park.*
·*Map: OS Explorer OL27, North York Moors East.*

Goathland is a breezy resort scattered on a green couch amid heather moors. The setting exudes healthiness, from St. Mary's church down to the station on the North Yorkshire Moors Railway. In between, houses and hotels stand back from an extensive common with stone causeys. At New Year you can witness the Plough Stots longsword dance team enact an ancient custom throughout the village. Goathland has been transformed into a tourist venue as Aidensfield, fictional 1960s home of long-running TV series *Heartbeat*: the *Goathland Hotel* doubles as the *Aidensfield Arms*. There are shops, Post office, tearooms and WC.

Descend the road to the station and cross the line to a gate onto the heathery foot of Goathland Moor. Take the path ascending sharp left outside the railway fence. At the top it runs on the edge of open moorland, outside the deep wooded valley. As Darnholme and the railway line appear, a steep, largely stone stepped descent is made to a lush open space, bridging a sidestream and on towards an enviably sited house. The path crosses Eller Beck on a footbridge to the left, to join the road which is followed right the few steps to its demise at another charming house.

Cross the stepping-stones, and in a few steps go left to a footbridge on a stream. From here a path makes a steep ascent then rises more gently through bracken. When the wall turns away, take a fence-stile and cross the field to join a drive to the house ahead. From the gate pass above the buildings to a bridle-gate onto bracken moorland. A green path heads away with a wall to a fork of inviting ways. Take that bearing left, quickly reaching a point above the steep slope revealing a waterfall on the beck far below. The broad grassy path slants down to a wall corner near the bottom. Below, the railway makes a double crossing of the beck. Your way advances straight on the moor bottom, past a cottage and on to Hill Farm. Bear left in front of it onto an access road, which drops down to meet a through road. Turn left over the rail bridge and steeply down into Beck Hole.

This sleepy hamlet boasts an enchanting setting: the *Birch Hall Inn* is a gem, and doubles as a small shop! The detour to Thomason Foss is made on a cul-de-sac path on the left just before the bridge. A grassy path ascends the open bank, then above a perilously steep drop to Eller Beck. It continues up to run briefly by the railway before steps down to the beck. A simple stroll upstream quickly reaches the craggy amphitheatre where the attractive waterfall spills into a clear pool. Up behind are rail viaduct arches.

Returning to Beck Hole go through a gate opposite, and a track runs downstream to the old railway, site of Beck Hole's station. Here the original horse-drawn tramway began its steep climb to Goathland, but its deficiencies resulted in the opening of a deviation line in 1865. The replacement track improved the gradient by starting its climb sooner, leaving Beck Hole station an early casualty. Go left over a footbridge on Eller Beck and on to Incline Cottage at the foot of the incline. A steady haul through wooded surrounds absorbs an access road just before reaching a road. Cross straight over and resume on a still rising grassy way, entering the village and finally levelling

4 miles   from Hunt House

A classic mixture of beckside and moorland walking.

• Start: Car park above Hunt House Farm, at end of
Hunt House Road which leaves Egton Bridge road
a short way west of Goathland (GR: 814989).
• Map: OS Explorer OL27, North York Moors East.

Advance along the continuing road just as far as
the entrance to Hunt House. At this very point double back
acutely left up the slope. Keen eyes might locate a narrow
path, but either way simply ascend to a large cairn on the
skyline above the bouldery edge. This stands on the edge
of a heather plateau, and a clear path heads off to the left.

The path contours atop the diminishing line of
modest rock outcrops high above the road, largely on the
boundary between bracken slope below and heather to the
right. This course is maintained for some time, passing fre-
quent sizeable cairns. A fork is reached just before a
scrappy cairn on a large, flat-topped boulder. The left
branch drops down to a moist dip, then on to meet the
broad path visible lower down. Better though to take the
right one, which remains higher to swing round and within a
minute reveal, with some surprise, a small sheet of water
called simply The Tarn. Set in a curious hollow and entirely
reed-fringed, it is actually artificial, having been created in
the 1920s for winter skating by damming a moss.

The path slants down above it to a ruinous sheep-
fold, Old Kit Bield, at the far end. Merging with another
path, cross the depression just beyond the tarn and over

the minor brow on the left. A gentle descent to Goathland is made, the village soon appearing to guide the way down. To the right are evidences of an old golf course, while there is a brief distant glimpse of the 'sandcastle' at RAF Fylingdales. Drop down past the square pinfold (which contains a tree planted in 1935 to commemorate the Silver Jubilee of King George V) to the road junction outside the *Mallyan Spout Hotel* (public bar).

Leave the road by an iron kissing-gate to the right of the hotel, from where a well-made path descends into the trees enclosing West Beck. Joining a beckside path at the bottom, turn left upstream. With care on potentially slippery boulders, this soon arrives at the fall of Mallyan Spout. An innocuous sidestream is the setting for this sometimes spectacular mini-series of cataracts.

Clamber over rocks to resume upstream, and a pair of footbridges links the path briefly onto the opposite bank. Occasionally muddy sections are a small price to pay for the outstanding wooded beck scenery (lively West Beck is formed by the merging of Wheeldale Beck and Wheeldale Gill). Beyond a stile the trees thin out but the beck remains a constant companion until reaching a stone arched bridge. Turn left up the road as far as a sharp bend left, then go right on a short drive to New Wath House, a pottery.

Continue past the house on a good moorland path above the intake wall to reach a fence corner. While the path goes straight ahead, first take the short detour to Nelly Ayre Foss. This turns right with the fence, then downstream a short way to view the falls reached by a short, steep bank. If uneasy on the slippery bank, simply view the modest fall from the bank top. Retrace steps to the fence corner, and turn right on the very inviting path which slants ever gradually over the low moor to meet Hunt House Road. Turn right on the grassy verge to finish.

4 miles   from Hunt House

**The environs of Wheeldale provide what would still
be a superb walk even without the highlight, an
outstanding march along a distinctive Roman road.**

•Start: *Car park above Hunt House Farm, at end of
Hunt House Road which leaves Egton Bridge road
a short way west of Goathland (GR: 814989).*
•Map: *OS Explorer OL27, North York Moors East.*

From the start look across the main valley to the
part wooded side valley directly opposite: this is Wheeldale
Gill, the first objective of the walk. Descend a rough road
immediately below the parking area, slanting down to a gate
off the moor and down to the bank of Wheeldale Beck.
Just yards downstream is its confluence with Wheeldale
Gill to form West Beck. If the concrete ford is impassable
then go left on a path linking footbridges over both becks
in succession, to a gate opposite the ford.

Ignore the bridleway downstream, and head off
on a broad grassy track across the field to a stile into
Hazel Head Woods. The path goes briefly left to join the
bank of Wheeldale Gill, then turns to follow it upstream.
This is a superb section of path running between the beck
and the plantation. At the end it emerges into the open just
short of the moorland road from Egton Bridge to Stape.

Turn left over a footbridge beneath the ford, and
head up the ample grass verges of the steep road. A wall
quickly joins in, and as the gradient eases continue for a
further mile amid the vast heathery sweep of Wheeldale

46

Moor. On the highest point, the Lyke Wake Walk challenge route crosses the road at right-angles. A little further, note a good example of a sheep bield, a stone shelter on the left. Descending the other side, Cropton Forest's remorselessly dark cloak fills the skyline ahead. Leave the road at a gate on the left as the fence turns off. Here the Roman Road is joined at an information panel.

Double sharply back left on the Roman road, unmissable from the outset. Its compelling company makes a splendid march, rising slightly then contouring across increasingly moor-like surrounds. About 16 feet wide, the road was uncovered early in the 20th century and is one of the best preserved in the country. Possibly leading to Roman signal stations along the coast near Whitby, it is also known as Wade's Causeway after a legendary local giant. The impressive stone slabbed surface has long intrigued historians, not all of whom attribute this to the Romans: it has been suggested it could even pre-date their occupation.

The road is vacated a little short of the wall ahead, but if suitably enthralled it is easy enough to advance further towards the wall and cut back on the Lyke Wake Walk, or even continue beyond the ladder-stile, where a further impressive length runs. The main option, however, is a broad branch path slanting right, down through heather to the steeper bank above Wheeldale Beck. It then absorbs the Lyke Wake Walk and drops down to the beck at some stepping-stones. Across the sturdy stones, rise through a gate then fork left off the Lyke Wake Walk (which ascends through the bracken in front), on the path rising by the fence to isolated Wheeldale Lodge. This former shooting lodge was a much-loved youth hostel from 1948 to 1999. Pass to its right and continue up its access road to meet the surfaced road end at Hunt House, with the start just a minute further.

HILLSIDE GUIDES... cover much of Northern England

Other *Pocket Walks* guides (more available shortly)
·WHARFEDALE, Yorkshire Dales
·AMBLESIDE & LANGDALE, Lake District

Our *Walking Country* range features more great walks...
·NORTH YORK MOORS, SOUTH (Rosedale & Farndale)
·NORTH YORK MOORS, WEST (Cleveland/Hambleton Hills)

·WHARFEDALE ·MALHAMDALE ·WENSLEYDALE
·SWALEDALE ·NIDDERDALE ·THREE PEAKS
·HOWGILL FELLS ·TEESDALE ·EDEN VALLEY

·ILKLEY MOOR ·BRONTE COUNTRY ·CALDERDALE
·BOWLAND ·PENDLE & RIBBLE ·WEST PENNINE MOORS

·SOUTHERN PENNINES ·NORTHERN PEAK ·EASTERN PEAK
·CENTRAL PEAK ·SOUTHERN PEAK ·WESTERN PEAK

·LAKELAND FELLS, SOUTH ·LAKELAND FELLS, EAST
·LAKELAND FELLS, NORTH ·LAKELAND FELLS, WEST

Long Distance Walks, including
·CLEVELAND WAY ·DALES WAY ·LADY ANNE'S WAY
·COAST TO COAST WALK ·TRANS-PENNINE WAY

Also available
·YORKSHIRE DALES VISITOR GUIDE
·YORKSHIRE DALES, MOORS & FELLS
·THE HIGH PEAKS OF ENGLAND & WALES

Visit www.hillsidepublications.co.uk
or write for a catalogue